The Narcissist's Playbook

How to Neutralize and Outmaneuver Manipulative Individuals

Linda R. Sloan

Copyright © Linda R. Sloan, 2023

All rights reserved. No part of this publication may be reproduced, distributed, or transmitted in any form or by any means, including photocopying, recording, or other electronic or mechanical methods, without the prior written permission of the publisher, except in the case of brief quotations embodied in critical reviews and certain other noncommercial uses permitted by copyright law.

Table of Contents

Chapter 1: Understanding Narcissism 5
    Definition of Narcissism 6
    Characteristics of a Narcissist 7
    Causes of Narcissism 13

Chapter 2: Red Flags to Watch Out For 16
    Assessing the Level of Narcissism 17

Chapter 3: Managing a Narcissist in Your Life 23
    Dealing with manipulation and gaslighting 25
    Strategies for maintaining sanity 27

Chapter 4: Protecting Yourself from Narcissistic Abuse 30
    Identifying and Escaping Abusive Situations 32
    Healing from Narcissist trauma 33

Chapter 5: Moving Forward 35
    Building a Support System 35
    Building Your Self-Esteem 36
    Finding Joy and Happiness in Life After narcissism ... 36

Chapter 1: Understanding Narcissism

Narcissism is a personality disorder characterized by an inflated sense of self-importance, a need for admiration, and a lack of empathy for others. Narcissists believe they are superior to others and often have grandiose fantasies of success, power, or attractiveness. They also tend to be manipulative and exploit others for their own gain.

There are several theories about the causes of narcissism. Some experts believe it may be due to childhood experiences, such as being overly praised or not receiving enough attention or validation. Others attribute it to genetic factors or brain abnormalities.

It's important to note that not all individuals who display narcissistic traits have a full-blown personality disorder. Narcissistic traits can range from mild to severe and may be present in different degrees in different people. However, individuals with severe narcissistic traits may experience significant difficulties in their personal and professional relationships and may benefit from therapy or other forms of treatment.

Definition of Narcissism

Narcissism is a personality disorder that is classified in the Diagnostic and Statistical Manual of Mental Disorders (DSM-5) as a "Cluster B" personality disorder. It is characterized by an exaggerated sense of self-importance, a need for admiration and attention, and a lack of empathy for others. Narcissists often believe that they are superior to others and may have grandiose fantasies of success, power, or attractiveness.

Characteristics of a Narcissist

There are several characteristics that are commonly associated with narcissism. These include:

An inflated sense of self-importance: Narcissists often have an exaggerated sense of their own importance and may believe that they are superior to others. This may manifest in a number of ways, such as constantly boasting about their accomplishments or expecting to be treated as a special or unique individual. Narcissists may also have an unrealistic sense of their own abilities and may overestimate their competence or intelligence. This sense of self-importance can lead narcissists to act entitled or arrogant and may cause them to dismiss or belittle the opinions or feelings of others. It can also make them resistant to criticism or feedback, as they may see it as a threat to their ego or status.

A need for admiration: Narcissists often seek out attention and admiration from others and may become upset or angry if they do not receive it. They may constantly seek validation from others and may become overly concerned with their appearance or status in order to gain admiration. This need for admiration may lead narcissists to engage in attention-seeking behaviors, such as constantly seeking praise or attention from others or trying to dominate conversations. It may also lead them to become jealous or envious of others who receive praise or attention that they feel they deserve. The constant need for admiration can be exhausting for those around the narcissist and may lead to strained relationships

A lack of empathy: Narcissists may have difficulty understanding or caring about the feelings of others. They may be indifferent to the suffering or needs of others and may exploit them for their own gain. This lack of empathy may be evident in their interactions with others, as they may not show concern or compassion when others are in need or are experiencing hardship. They may also be insensitive to the feelings of others and may not consider the impact of their actions on others. This lack of empathy can make it difficult for narcissists to form close, meaningful relationships with others and may lead to conflicts or misunderstandings in their interactions.

Manipulative behavior: Narcissists may use manipulation tactics such as gaslighting or lying to get what they want or to make others feel inferior. Gaslighting is a form of manipulation in which the manipulator seeks to make the victim question their own perceptions or memories by denying or altering the truth. Narcissists may use this tactic to deflect blame, create confusion, or maintain control over a situation or person. They may also lie or deceive others in order to get what they want or to protect their own ego. This manipulative behavior can be harmful to those around the narcissist and may lead to strained or toxic relationships.

A sense of entitlement: Narcissists may feel entitled to special treatment or privileges and may become upset or angry if they do not receive it. They may expect others to cater to their needs or demands and may become entitled or demanding if these expectations are not met. This sense of entitlement may be evident in their interactions with others, as they may expect preferential treatment or may become angry or resentful if they do not receive it. This entitlement can lead to conflicts or misunderstandings in their relationships with others and may make it difficult for narcissists to form close, meaningful connections with others

Splitting:The narcissist's personality is divided between good and terrible portions, and they also separate everything in their relationships into good and bad.

Any unpleasant ideas or actions are blamed on you or others, yet they take credit for anything that is wonderful and excellent.

They deny their unpleasant comments and deeds while repeatedly blaming you of disapproving.

They also recall things as fully nice and amazing or as dreadful and horrible. They can't seem to blend these two conceptions.

A few instances of a narcissist's separating conduct in action: Marty declared the entire trip wrecked and the worst ever since the hotel room didn't fulfill his expectations and the weather wasn't great.

A man was blamed for 20 years since he wasn't there when his wife delivered their first kid even though he was delayed in Chicago.

Vicky's husband rejected her reservations about the $20,000 cost for the new landscaping since he liked it.

Narcissists aren't able to perceive, feel, or recall both the great and the bad in a circumstance. They can cope with just one viewpoint at a time.

Perceiving everything as a threat
Although they're extremely attentive to perceived threats, rage, and rejection from others, narcissists usually mistake minor facial signals and are generally predisposed toward viewing facial expressions as negative.

Unless you are acting out your feelings strongly, the narcissist won't correctly comprehend what you're experiencing.

Even expressing "I'm sorry" or "I love you" while the narcissist is on edge and furious might backfire. They won't believe you and may even misperceive your statement as an assault.

if your words and expressions aren't consistent, the narcissist may likely reply erroneously or become defensive.

This is why narcissists sometimes misunderstand sarcasm as true agreement or joking from others as a personal assault.

The lack of capacity to accurately interpret body language, a prevalent narcissist feature, is one reason narcissists are deficiently sensitive to your emotions.

They don't notice them, they don't interpret them appropriately, and ultimately they don't think you feel any differently than they do.

Causes of Narcissism

There are several theories about the causes of narcissism, but the exact cause is not fully understood. Some experts believe that narcissistic traits may be due to childhood experiences, such as being overly praised or not receiving enough attention or validation.

Other causes Include

Environment – parent-child connections with either too much admiration or too much criticism that don't reflect the child's real experiences and accomplishments.

Genetics – hereditary qualities, such as specific personality traits.

Neurobiology – the relationship between the brain and behavior and thinking.

Chapter 2: Red Flags to Watch Out For

Here are a few red flags to watch out for when interacting with someone who may be a narcissist:

They are very self-centered and only think about their own needs and wants.
They exaggerate their accomplishments and talents.
They have a sense of entitlement and believe they deserve special treatment.
They have difficulty empathizing with others and may be indifferent to others' feelings.

They may manipulate or exploit others to get what they want.
They may have an unstable or volatile personality, with sudden mood swings or outbursts of anger.
A lack of willingness to compromise or take responsibility in relationships.
A tendency to be envious of others or to believe that others are envious of them.

A lack of remorse or guilt for harmful actions.
A tendency to manipulate or exploit others for their own gain.
A preoccupation with fantasies of power, success, and attractiveness.

Assessing the Level of Narcissism

There are several ways to access the level of narcissism in an individual. One method is to use self-report measures, in which the person completes a questionnaire or interview that asks about their thoughts, feelings, and behaviors. Some commonly used self-report measures of narcissism include the Narcissistic Personality Inventory (NPI) and the Hypersensitive Narcissism Scale (HSNS).

Another way to assess narcissism is through observation and interview. This can be done by trained professionals, such as psychologists or psychiatrists, who can look for signs of narcissistic behavior and thought patterns during a clinical evaluation. The different types of Narcissist are

Grandiose narcissism: This type is characterized by an inflated sense of self-importance, a need for admiration, and a lack of empathy. Grandiose narcissists may have a grand vision of themselves and their place in the world, and they may engage in risky or reckless behavior in pursuit of their goals.

Vulnerable narcissism: This type is characterized by a fragile ego and a deep sense of insecurity. Vulnerable narcissists may be more sensitive to criticism and may try to compensate for their insecurities through aggressive or defensive behavior.

Malignant narcissism: This type is characterized by a combination of grandiose and vulnerable narcissism, as well as a lack of empathy and a willingness to exploit or manipulate others for personal gain. Malignant narcissists may engage in aggressive or abusive behavior and may show a lack of remorse or guilt for their actions.

Cerebral narcissism: This type is characterized by an emphasis on intelligence and achievement, and a belief that these qualities are the most important indicators of worth. Cerebral narcissists may be preoccupied with their own intellectual pursuits and may view others as inferior if they do not measure up.

Somatic narcissism: This type is characterized by an emphasis on physical appearance and sexual attractiveness, and a belief that these qualities are the most important indicators of worth. Somatic narcissists may be preoccupied with their own appearance and may view others as inferior if they do not meet their standards of attractiveness.

Exploitative narcissism: This type is characterized by a desire to dominate and control others, and a willingness to use manipulation or coercion to achieve these ends. Exploitative narcissists may take advantage of others for their own benefit and may have a lack of concern for the well-being of those they exploit.

Exhibitionist narcissism: This type is characterized by a need for attention and a desire to be the center of attention. Exhibitionist narcissists may engage in attention-seeking behavior and may be prone to making grandiose statements or gestures in order to draw attention to themselves.

Collective narcissism: This type refers to a belief in the superiority of a group to which an individual belongs (such as a nation, race, or religion) and a desire to promote the greatness of the group. Collective narcissists may engage in discriminatory or aggressive behavior towards those outside of the group.

It's important to note that these types of narcissism are not mutually exclusive and an individual may exhibit traits from multiple types. It's also worth noting that narcissism exists on a spectrum, and not everyone who displays narcissistic traits meets the criteria for a diagnosis of narcissistic personality disorder.

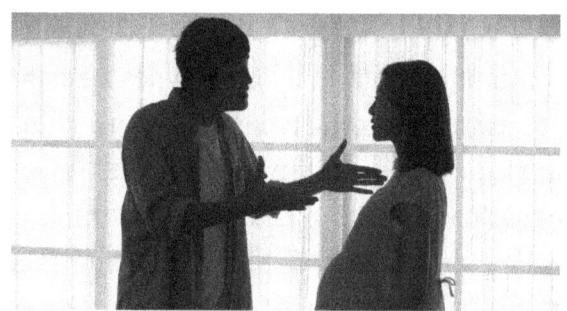

Chapter 3: Managing a Narcissist in Your Life

If you have a narcissist in your life, it can be challenging to navigate your relationship with them. Narcissists can be manipulative, controlling, and demanding, and it can be difficult to maintain your own sense of self and boundaries when dealing with them. However, there are some strategies you can use to manage your interactions with narcissists and protect yourself from their negative impact.

Set boundaries: It is important to establish and maintain clear boundaries with narcissists. This may mean saying no to unreasonable requests or setting limits on how much time you spend with them.

Communicate assertively: Stand up for yourself and express your needs and feelings in a direct and respectful manner. Avoid being confrontational or aggressive, as this may only escalate the situation.

Practice self-care: Take care of your own emotional and physical well-being by setting aside time for activities that nourish you and seeking support from friends and loved ones.

Seek outside help: If you are struggling to cope with a narcissist in your life, consider seeking the support of a mental health professional. A therapist can help you develop coping strategies and provide a safe space to process your emotions.

Limit contact: If the narcissist in your life is causing you significant distress, it may be necessary to limit or cut off contact with them. This can be a difficult decision, but it may be necessary for your own well-being.

Remember that it is not your responsibility to fix a narcissist or change their behavior. The most important thing is to take care of yourself and protect your own well-being.

Dealing with manipulation and gaslighting

Recognize the signs: It is important to be aware of the tactics that narcissists may use to manipulate and control you, such as gaslighting (manipulating you into doubting your own perception of reality), playing the victim, or using charm and charisma to get what they want.

Don't try to reason with them: Narcissists may be resistant to logic and reason and may try to twist your words or manipulate the conversation to suit their own needs. Don't get drawn into a debate or try to convince them of your perspective. Instead, focus on setting boundaries and asserting your own needs and feelings.

Document everything: Keep a record of conversations, requests, and any instances of manipulation or gaslighting. This can be helpful if you need to seek support or take legal action.

Protect yourself: Consider setting limits on your interactions with the manipulator and creating a plan for how to handle future instances of manipulation. It may also be necessary to cut off contact with the manipulator if they are causing significant harm to your well-being.

There are many different strategies that can be helpful for dealing with narcissists and managing your relationships with them. Here are a few more ideas:

Focus on your own feelings and needs: Remember that it is important to prioritize your own well-being and take care of yourself. This may mean saying no to unreasonable requests or setting limits on your interactions with the narcissist.

Don't personalize their behavior: Narcissists may say or do hurtful things in order to get what they want. It's important to remember that their behavior is about them, not about you. Try not to take their words or actions personally.

Seek therapy: If you are struggling to cope with a narcissistic relationship, consider seeking the support of a mental health professional. A therapist can help you develop coping strategies and provide a safe space to process your emotions.

Communicate assertively: Stand up for yourself and express your needs and feelings in a direct and respectful manner. Avoid being confrontational or aggressive, as this may only escalate the situation.

Strategies for maintaining sanity

Maintaining sanity can be challenging, especially in times of stress or uncertainty. Here are some strategies that may help:

Take breaks: Make sure to take breaks from work or other tasks and do something that you enjoy. This can help you relax and recharge.

Stay active: Engaging in physical activity, such as going for a walk or doing yoga, can help you stay physically and mentally healthy.

Stay connected: Maintain connections with friends and family, either in person or through phone or video calls. Having a supportive social network can help you feel less isolated and provide a sense of belonging.

Get enough sleep: Make sure to get enough sleep each night. Lack of sleep can contribute to feelings of stress and anxiety.

Practice relaxation techniques: There are many relaxation techniques that can help you manage stress, such as deep breathing, meditation, or progressive muscle relaxation.

Eat a healthy diet: A healthy diet that includes a variety of fruits, vegetables, and whole grains can help improve your mood and energy levels.

Practice gratitude: Focusing on the things you are grateful for can help you maintain a positive outlook and improve your mental well-being.

Seek out new experiences: Engaging in new activities or trying something new can help you stay engaged and motivated, and can also provide a sense of accomplishment.

Find ways to manage stress: There are many ways to manage stress, such as practicing mindfulness, getting regular exercise, or finding a hobby that you enjoy.

Take care of your physical health: Maintaining good physical health, such as through regular exercise and getting enough sleep, can help improve your mental health

Chapter 4: Protecting Yourself from Narcissistic Abuse

Narcissistic abuse is a form of emotional abuse that is perpetrated by individuals who have a narcissistic personality disorder. These individuals are characterized by an inflated sense of self-importance, a need for admiration, and a lack of empathy for others. They often use manipulative tactics to control and exploit the people around them, including those closest to them, such as their romantic partners, family members, and friends. If you are in a relationship with a narcissist, or if you have encountered a narcissistic individual in some other context, it is important to know how to protect yourself from their abusive behavior. Here are some tips for protecting yourself from narcissistic abuse:

Educate yourself about narcissistic personality disorder and abusive behavior. Understanding the dynamics of narcissistic abuse can help you recognize it when it is happening and give you the tools to respond effectively.

Know when to seek help. If the narcissistic abuse is severe or you feel unsafe, it may be necessary to seek help from a trusted authority figure or to leave the relationship.

Avoid engaging in personal attacks or trying to "win" arguments with a narcissist. Narcissists often try to provoke a reaction from their victims in order to maintain control, so it is important to stay calm and avoid getting drawn into their tactics.

Seek legal protection if necessary. In some cases, narcissistic abuse may involve physical violence or threats of violence. If this is the case, it may be necessary to seek a restraining order or other legal protection.

Don't blame yourself. It is common for victims of narcissistic abuse to blame themselves for the behavior of the narcissist. However, it is important to remember that the narcissist's behavior is their responsibility, and you are not to blame.

Identifying and Escaping Abusive Situations

Narcissistic abuse is a specific type of emotional abuse that is perpetrated by individuals with narcissistic personality disorder. Narcissistic abusers often engage in a range of abusive behaviors, including belittling, manipulating, and gaslighting their victims. It is important to recognize the signs of narcissistic abuse so that you can take steps to protect yourself and seek help.

Some signs of narcissistic abuse include:

Your partner belittles or humiliates you in front of others or privately.
Your partner manipulates or gaslights you, making you doubt your own perceptions and memories.
Your partner controls your access to money, transportation, or other resources.

Your partner is physically violent or abusive towards you.
Your partner forces you to have sex or engage in sexual activities that you are not comfortable with.

Healing from Narcissist trauma

Narcissistic trauma refers to the psychological injuries that can result from a relationship with a narcissistic person. These injuries can be deeply wounding and long-lasting, and they can interfere with a person's ability to have healthy, fulfilling relationships in the future. If you have experienced narcissistic trauma, it is important to seek out support and take steps to heal. Here are some tips that may be helpful in your journey of recovery:

Practice forgiveness: Forgiveness does not mean condoning the harmful behavior of the narcissistic person, but it can be an important step in the healing process. Forgiveness can help you let go of anger and resentment and move forward in a healthy way

Another important aspect of healing from narcissistic trauma is learning to recognize and challenge the negative thought patterns that can arise as a result of abuse. These may include beliefs about yourself being unworthy or undeserving of love and respect.

Chapter 5: Moving Forward

It is indeed possible to move forward after a narcissistic relationship, but it can be a challenging process. Narcissistic individuals can be manipulative and can cause emotional damage to their partners, Here are some steps you can take to help you move forward:

Building a Support System

Building a supportive network can provide you with emotional support, understanding, and guidance as you navigate the challenges of recovering from a narcissistic relationship. It can be helpful to have a network of people you can turn to for advice, encouragement, and a listening ear. A support system can also provide you with a sense of community and belonging, which can be especially important when you're healing from a difficult experience.

Building Your Self-Esteem

Building self-esteem is an important step in recovering from a narcissistic relationship because narcissistic abuse can take a toll on your self-worth and confidence. It's important to work on rebuilding your self-esteem so that you can move forward in a healthy, positive way.

Finding Joy and Happiness in Life After narcissism

It's important to recognize that moving on from a narcissistic relationship and finding joy and happiness in life is a process that takes time. It's normal to have ups and downs, and to have moments where you feel discouraged or overwhelmed. Here are some additional tips that may help you:

Take things one day at a time: It's okay to take things slowly and to focus on just getting through the day. You don't have to solve all of your problems at once.

Seek out healthy relationships: Surrounding yourself with supportive, healthy people can make a big difference in your healing journey. It can be helpful to build a network of friends and family who can provide emotional support and encouragement.

Seek closure: If possible, try to find closure in the relationship. This may involve having a conversation with the narcissist or simply coming to terms with what happened in your own mind.

Find healthy ways to cope: It's important to find healthy ways to cope with your emotions. This may include talking to a therapist, practicing mindfulness, or finding healthy outlets like exercise or creative expression.

Set goals: Having goals to work towards can give you a sense of purpose and help you move forward. These goals can be big or small, but make sure they are meaningful to you

Engage in activities that bring you joy: Identify the things that bring you happiness and make an effort to incorporate them into your life. This could be hobbies, sports, volunteering, or anything else that brings you joy.

Practice gratitude: Focusing on the things you are thankful for can help shift your perspective and bring more positivity into your life. Try keeping a gratitude journal or sharing your gratitude with others.

Learn from the past: It can be helpful to reflect on your experience with narcissism and try to understand what happened. This can help you learn from the past and move forward in a healthy way.

www.ingramcontent.com/pod-product-compliance
Lightning Source LLC
Chambersburg PA
CBHW050323220526
45465CB00005B/2111